Dying in Love

by

Patrick Ellis

Edited by Susannah Ellis

Chevalier Publishing

Published by

Chevalier Publishing
27 Church Road
Newton Abbot
Devon TQ12 1AL

chevalierpublishing@brandan.co.uk

Printed and bound in Great Britain by
Antony Rowe Ltd, Chippenham, Wiltshire

ISBN 0 9544293 0 3

for
gus

Introduction

Words have always been my food. They pour from my dreams, my thoughts, my mouth, my fingertips, as though I have tried to tame them and they must break free. Each experience, each transient moment can be recorded upon a page and made eternal, allowed to survive beyond the human restrictions of our memories and their recollection. To transcribe language is to photograph a sound, a smell, the gold that follows daybreak: to mould the form of a moment through the written medium is to hold a paintbrush over a blank canvas and replicate reality.

And then, even beyond this, there is poetry.

It offers us more than suggestion, more than ideas and concepts. It walks us down an avenue into its own dimension, immodest in its intimacy, stipulating nothing except possibility whilst offering all: a place that not only speaks of our past and our present but holds the clues to what we are yet to be.

Perhaps we ache to awaken the poetry sleeping in ourselves, and so we reach for the beauty of another's. The joy for me in Patrick collating some of his work and publishing this collection of poetry is that I can now reach for his. Sometime right back in the beginning of this process, he remarked, with eyes wide with incredulity, that it would be a mystery to him anyone choosing to read his ramblings, let alone buying them! And yet, it may be that very quality which defines the power of his words. He writes to understand his experiences, not to master the act of their literary creation; seeking answers and not endeavouring to deliver them.

For if experiences were the air we breathe in and words were our breaths released, poetry would be our lungs.

Simone Chevalier

Acknowledgements

France, 2002

It is difficult to thank all those who have been instrumental in my journey through this life, but to the following people I owe more than I can ever repay. My friend Tom Welch, who has been my sounding board during our many long walks and long talks in the woods, a man of true strength and great wisdom. Katrina, my friend and first teacher of Self, who has always bestowed such searing insights and unwavering support. My mother, whose enthusiasm and *joie de vivre* brings a smile to all she meets and whose selfless love of me has always been my blessing. And my sister, who has the biggest heart I have ever known, and whose love and generosity of Spirit have been a rock to lean against and safely rest a while throughout my life.

But this simple little book of the wanderings of my mind through certain experiences that have shaped me as a man, would not, indeed could not, have happened without my daughter, Susannah, and the unquenchable belief in my words she somehow possesses. This extraordinary, gifted woman, with more talent than I could ever dream about and more beauty than she will perhaps ever realise, has been a light shining brightly in my life since the moment she was born. Without her encouragement, sensitivity and perception, and her untiring editorial help, I would not have dared made public these private scribblings, written just for me to make sense of some of the potent moments that have brought me here. I love you, precious heart, and without you my life would have no meaning at all.

Deeply, I thank each of you for choosing *me* to love.

Patrick Ellis

'The heart is measured by how much *you* love
not how much you are loved by others.'

Somehow

From passion's blueprints we imagine a future, shaping its form using tools crafted with devotion, and we believe time is on our side. And then the sea rolls in and the castle falls. In intimate relationship two experiences compose the completeness of one, but neither person is ever truly able to walk uninvolved through the other's perspective. And thus the loneliness of love's finality.

and may became november
somehow

and minutes became months
somehow

as we danced this dance
of you and me

time passed in clusters of belly-backed bliss
wedged by weeks of wanting and waiting
until,
in a shooting-star-second
you were gone

our thoughts became the plans
that manifest dreams
now just the remains
of fading fantasies
as life wrenched you,
hardly struggling,
from us

my head throbs
with thoughts of you,
each second bubble-gum-stretched
from candle-lit skin petal-clothed
to this pit of sorrow
as you tiptoe and trample through
what's left of me

it was impossible i know, i know
but it's all so savagely real still
as i smell the smell of you,

somehow

Living Love

Love. The great adventure. It is only in the polarities of human love do we truly experience the totality of love. How would we know pleasure if we have not experienced pain; how would we know joy if we have not experienced its absence? We cannot just take the wonderful aspects of being in love and expect it to be without those negative times where we question its very presence. How many times do we hold love responsible when the responsibility is purely ours?

What do I know of love?

this rare jewel in my life
this heart's constant duellist
this delicious pleasure
this deepest pain
this wondrous high
this desperate hole

What do I see of love?

the laughing eyes
the cutting words
the excited plans
the brutal truth
the tender touch
the frozen silence

What do I feel of love?

its fervent strength
its fearful retreat
its magical birth
its empty end
its selfless courage
its mean indifference

What can I tell you of love?

Love does not lie, it is lied to.
It is not love that hurts or destroys.
We use it as if we own it,
as if it's ours to give or take.

We crush it with fear and anger and jealousy
and blame it when it breaks.

Slagheap

When we love someone, who for any one of a hundred reasons is unable to love us or stay with us, and eventually leaves, we are left with the overwhelming sense of our own worthlessness. For when we have offered our entirety and it is renounced, self-beliefs become exchanged for doubts in the onslaught of the loss of our emotional identity.

I feel used up and tossed aside
an empty milk carton on a refuse tip
ripped and battered,
a sad reminder of its former life

I have given and given
and given again
yet it never seems enough
and how could it be?
how could I be?

and as the slagheap of my emotions sags and decays
all horizons disappear
dreams dissolve,
only illusions stare back
unblinking

I have tried and tried
and tried again
but it never seems enough
and how could it be?
how could I be?

the future is a black hole of uncertainty
I am shrink-wrapped by the
nothingness of everything
a mummified memory staggering
into an unforgiving void

I have loved and loved
and loved again
yet it never seems enough
and how could it be?

how could I be?

Mysteries

When we search for a love that encapsulates all spiritual, emotional and sexual dimensions, we build a pedestal in the sky of our desires and place love upon it. Love becomes ideal, true only when it can climb its throne, an impossible concept that can only fall out of reach of those who try. For in defining love we somehow overlook its humanness, choosing to forget the humanity of the very vehicle through which we are able to express the beauty of our souls, the passion in our hearts. And in letting this knowledge slip away, undetected, the imbalance in our interpretations of love has us searching for angels.

When I think of you, I smile
A private smile that cannot be explained
For unless they have loved an angel
They could not understand

You slide beneath my skin
Where the warmth of you strokes my heart
Until the loss of you
Floods back

Reflection brings your shadow
To swoop and play and torment my mind
Only to turn and disappear
To a place still unknown to me

Each stone, each rounded hill
Each drop of holy water and every Hawthorn tree
Harpoons me to that place wherein you lie
Inside my core

I cannot climb the sacred Tor with you not there
Avalon embraces me, but without you
Reminds me only
Of joy once felt

You are not here always, you understand
You do not enter my dreams, that I am aware
Although I suspect you do
Were I just to remember

How do you tell them you love an angel?
Who would believe my loving you
Through many changing forms
Through Time and Space?

You would believe me
But then,
You already know

Angel on Morphine

Our own pain grants us with an appreciation and a little more understanding of another's, and enables us to journey with them a few steps closer to their place of healing. But occasionally we must accept that their life is their own and we cannot live it for them, though they may walk a precarious path towards the cliff's edge. In this inevitability we become as powerless as they are.

sweet fragile butterfly shaking at my door
the dead of night haloes your escape
from misery
to misery,
Vodka's bottled serum purges truth
but adopts pain in every pause,
pale lifeless eyes on some lost horizon
as the Valium numbness quells the storm

an occasional spark of who is still there
buried deep beneath a wrecked sense of self,
and a faint trace of whom you once were
behind glazed eyes and skin pitted by addiction,
your beauty hinting even now
though softly
since all the props and rich men's traps
collapsed beneath you

too frightened to live
as I was too keen to die,
I recognise the barren moonscape
of Death's waiting room
where you reside, barely alive,
but I chose to live
you choose to die

so this is goodbye, butterfly
your last tragic flight begins tonight,
the inner chaos veiling
the fuse lit long ago

just know, I cupped your dying heart
in conscious hands

Feather

When we are in the full flush of new love, all life becomes a magnificent painting and we become the artist. Our whole existence is magnified, every emotion heightened as love spreads from the relationship to encompass our whole life. It is this power of love that makes it so irresistible and, sometimes, so addictive.

freedom's desire slips silently away
as love's liberty moulds our form,
just an irrelevance amidst adulation
of this divine largesse

as razor love reveals Goddess lips of
tumescent anticipation,
a moist, unfolding Venus
glides me in and beyond bliss
to lay in awe of this beneficence

witnessing your wonder of life,
the belly-laughing,
feeling the fierce force of your dreams,
my emotions surge and swim around me
with dolphin grace and power
in this irresistible cadeau

my lady,
I flower you with velvet petals,
colour you with Picasso's brush,

and feather you

feather you

Judged

Our truth so often feels like the only truth when we stand too close to appreciate the view from another's perspective. For truth is truth, and everyone's truth is real to them, no matter how incomprehensible it may seem to us at the time. In judging others by our own concepts of right and wrong we pass opinions that not only fluctuate with the evolvement of our experiences, but which are also frequently driven by our emotional needs.

Imagine a world where everyone listened to each other and tried to understand their respective points of view? In that world anger and resentment would have no place to breed, for in understanding each other we understand more about us all.

Anger and confusion wrestle with my mind,
Just as trust and truth live in my heart.
Our yesterday was not all my doing,
Just part,
As today is and tomorrow coming.
My experiences carved the shape you fear,
The shape you love, as well, you say,
Then perhaps these shoes need walking in
Before you deem them so ill-worn.

You wound too.
When the sword's cause is just, you claim,
And without remorse, or so it seems,
Yet my wounds ache just as yours
And I scream pain just as you,
But in a different way.

I feel condemned by you, without appeal,
Dismissed by you as if diseased,
Belittled, as you peer upon my muddy path
From your oh-so-wise road.
Judge not, you say, as you judge me,
You call for truth yet humour mine,
And you cry for love
But where could there be love to equal yours?

Not here, you scorn.

I disagree.
'Tis just the form, is all.

Shooting Star

Choosing to be alone can seem a solution to the angst of a relationship or the trials of life, and indeed there are wonderful lessons to be learned from solitude. But the time comes when a certain person appears and shows us just how small our world has become, how great is our need to laugh and cry and feel. People are our gift, but a gift too easily forgotten in our natural avoidance of life's deepest challenges.

dancing and singing and laughing and crying,
like a shooting star in a clear coal sky
you burst upon my solitude,
and I stood bewitched, half-caught
betwixt belief and a trick of the night.

the joy that colours your eyes hides
the throbbing lies,
but you dove into the private lake of me
without a backwards glance of doubt:
a warrior returning from a distant war
hauling trophies of defeated foe
and beliefs of conquests made.

as you play and probe and tickle and tease,
rant and rage when the demons leave,
your emotions swim in a pool of truth:
the wondrous power of your Womanhood
in which you bathe.

reign no more those fears of despair!
no place survives for their damage done,
save in empathy for a traveller too,
a soul like you, with an open wound
to close.

the gift you gave that night
was missing from my life,
yet somewhere deep in
the soul of you
knew my need,
to see a shooting star
come burst upon my solitude.

Mouth

When lust exists by itself, most thoughts and desires remain unshared and the rawness of physical pleasure takes control. In many ways, and sometimes at best, a mutual masturbation takes place in some gratifying parade of prowess. It is loveless because love is not sought; it is empty because love is not present.

A shiver of excitement skips down his spine as
Her tongue teases a tensed thigh,
Blood pumps his hardness expectantly
And from her mouth slips a swallowed sigh.

Pleasure seeps though him,
Her tongue snailing its wetness towards his groin,
Rigid now, desiring her flirting mouth around
Flexed sinew, amidst a rumbling, hungry loin.

She cups him softy in perceptive hands,
And he waits, for the moment draws nigh,
When the softness of her mouth at last
Meets the rigour of his manhood's lie.

Twisting his head to one side
And holding a quietly panting breath,
His body urges her to consume him,
Savouring the ascent to fleeting orgasmic death.

His buttocks tighten, taughtness twitching
As she flicks his rounded tip, licks his length,
Gasping, as she intuitly draws him in,
Gripping with her practised, frightened strength.

con.

The warm, velvet wetness of her mouth
Releases spinning, spiralling shudders of desire,
As she rhythmically slides up and down,
Deeper and faster, higher and higher.

He reaches out to feel her moistness,
Parts her lips to touch the silky measure,
A stifled groan from far away avoids his fingers:
It is his moment, to receive. To take his pleasure.

Her mouth more purposeful now, her lips devour,
From his throat escape aroused but silent cries,
And as his muscles strain and twist,
Deep within he feels the familiar rise, and rise.

And with every sense heightened, defined, alive,
His mind becomes focused on her intimate kiss,
Time and thought disappear in his selfish surrender
To this loveless encounter with physical bliss.

Purple Kiss

One of the most extraordinary aspects of love, be it of another person or of Love in its spiritual form, is the connectedness you feel to all things. The smallest event, a butterfly flying close to you, a 'coincidence', a shared thought only later found to have been formed at the same time, become signs so meaningful they fall like confetti on your heart.

Perhaps in this state of love, or Love, we are indeed connected to our higher selves, experiencing that which is available all of the time and yet so frequently blunted by the materialistic nature of our human lives.

the light

oh, the light weaves through you

jade green purple silken flutterings

adrift in golden sunlight

harbinger of soul secrets

mellifluous messenger of middle love

tell me,

fragile ethereal seraphim,

what tidings do your wings embrace?

or are you she?

transmuting time

shifting shape

slipping through realities

to seal this heart with a butterfly kiss

Ghosts

How completely do we ever really know somebody, how much of this person we love still stands behind the fragile veils of insecurity and vulnerability? We are all so complex, so intricately woven, the fibres of our cloth so manifold, and yet the face of love looks into our depths, braves the labyrinth of our hidden fears, whilst its hands reach to untie the remnants of damage still strangling our inner lives.

To entrust our fears and vulnerabilities and to be entrusted with another's, is surely to be graced by the gentlest and deepest aspect of love.

I try to imagine the thoughts those doe eyes hide,
What wanderings go on behind
Smiles flashed
At strangers,
Lazy, liquid conversations with friends,
Or when tortured hands are held
And gentle, whispered words caress another's pain.
I wonder who speaks to you
When you are alone,
And what you hear them say.
My worry bids me linger
By the dark alleys in which you stumble,
The head-banged walls you try to break through,
Silently beating old ghosts away.

Let me be a candle to light the shadows of your fears,
A bowl of scented water to wash away the tattooed wrongs,
A feather brush to clear the cobwebs of crippling beliefs,
A silk bandage to bind those still-so-seeping wounds.

But, most of all,
Let my love for you be your sanctuary,
A place to rest and hide awhile
From all that hurts
And all that harms.

Always

Our prayers frequently seem to go unanswered, but when you have experienced God in any of the forms He manifests, or by any of the names we like to attach to Her, when we have had contact with our higher selves, our Spiritual selves, we know our prayers are heard. If we can believe this, understand this to be true, then we are able to trust what happens is meant to happen, that there is a reason and a timing for everything. And in *that* trust, freedom waits.

They do not speak
But we hear Them.
Unable to touch us
We feel Their embrace.
With our eyes closed,
We see Them.

There is no distance
Their Love cannot bridge;
No problem
Their Love does not solve;
Not one pain
They will not soothe.

Never again can loneliness
Grasp your heart,
When you know you are gently held
Within timeless Hands.

And when you trust in that Place
Wherein they wait,
You will know that they have been with you,

Always.

Survivors

We are all survivors of something. We have all suffered pain in some way; it is merely the degrees and our responses that diverge. If we could just change our mindset, realise more perceptively that we are all trying to do the best we can, not only are we then able to empathise with others but we can really begin to heal our own anguish. For some survivors become so trapped in *their* own suffering, it takes over their lives and corrupts their ability to understand another's. And in so doing we close ourselves to the healing touch of awareness.

with a rush buried emotions gush,
your death, then,
of a heart too-long anaesthetised
by the clan's stinging needles
and a sick stranger's prick.

as you struggle for air,
cagily raise your head
from another's pit of paranoia,
you breathe an escapee's freedom breath,
but abrasively,
avenging with bitter words,
daring me to fail
as all the others have done.

so beware,
for as the tides of resentment rise
another pit awaits, seducing,
usurping ancient submission
with soft-spoken cynical doubt.

I am not the enemy,
not me,
nor a saviour no more,
or an unwilling adversary to settle your score.

I am just a survivor, too.

This Love

Perhaps one of the grandest demonstrations of love is when we nourish the greater good of another in place of our own. To let someone go from your life when it offers them a freedom otherwise lessened by them staying, is to experience both the power and the powerlessness of loving so deeply. For it is when we move beyond the agony of our hearts we find the stillness of our higher selves and the true gifts of love.

If we could only realise earlier love has a courage unlike any other.

and the wind whispers words
of love to me
wild love to me,
the unspoken love
of this love

is that your heart i hear
brushing my ear
with a dragonfly-breath
of such soft caress
or my own?

i dismiss the longing
turn the page
heave my heart away,
but the wind weaves the words
of your gentle heart
and purple soul,
incandescent eyes, child wise
though almost weeping in the pain
of this love

i'd wondered why
lovers feed on scraps of love
grabbed and eaten
swallowed in emptiness
unfinished unfulfilled,
yet now i eat from your table
gratefully sucking the slice
of you
i'm granted in this love

i want to go with you
to where the truth is shown
in cloudless clarity, our feet
in crystal streams
of dreams
hands entwined, divined
lips on lips
at the sacred waist
of this love   con.

and the wind wrestles words
to this place where you are not

and reminds me who i am.

only
when the winds of wounds
cease to blow
and the past slinks away,
is this love left free to fly
untied

it rides the eagle's wing
and soars above the constant roar
of life
gliding on currents
of warm aired love
gazing down on people unlike us,
bemused

we were
we are
we will be again
know this to be true,
for our place of love is both
a memory
and
a vision
nothing can diminish

go live your life's dream
suck the sauce of freedom
taste the many flavoured dishes of desire

but know you are loved

limitlessly

Reflections

If each of us were to draw every breath from love, the world would soon become an environment of truth and acceptance. As individuals, we would no longer need to sacrifice being seen for hiding the face of our fears. But until the time comes where we fully integrate all the conflicting parts of ourselves and still our self-abusive tongues, we will go on censoring our shadows, hiding our believed unsightliness behind enigmatic screens.

In the candle as She looks,
Through leaping golden shards
Memory's flickering images flow.
Her eyes with the flame mould slowly into one,
Slipping away
From a world She barely understands.

As She becomes the fire,
Sits painted by an angel's brush,
She watches the child She was, spinning freely,
Dancing innocence in the multicoloured flare.
But another image catches Her eye, the same child
With frightened eyes,
Bathing in the burn of fear and loneliness,
Masked yet aching to be known -
The skipping smile the world sees
Hides this tear of living in the blur;
The part only She knows.

In the candle as She stares,
Mirrored by staccato slivers of light,
The woman She has become
Throws back Her mane of wild flowing hair,
Swirls Her flaring dress, and to unheard music
Wheels and whirls, twisting, turning
In a sensual, spiralling pirouette.
But as the dance slows, another figure is caught,
A woman's longing frozen in the sudden glare,
And fragile hands reach to veil a wounded heart
From the unwelcome gaze.

con.

Both sides of Herself unfold in the rainbow's play,
The side She shows and the side unseen
As trust and fear compete,
And as She unwinds from the waning flame and
The world around takes form again,
She knows both child and woman, unblemished and bruised,
Are Her;
The wonderful whole of Her.

No-one will watch as She hides a part,
Who will know if She acts a role,
Love comes when the shadow is nurtured as the spark:
The part only She sees.

No Blame

Blame confines us to being victims; forgiveness releases us. It is a complete healing process in its own right, embodying acceptance through acknowledgment and not denial. The effects from someone's treatment of us warrant responsibility, both by us and by them, though they may be unable or unwilling, and forgiveness then becomes an acceptance of the effects without the traps of blame.

This is crucial to all relationships, being equally pivotal for those who nurse someone they love over a great deal of time. For regardless then of the strength of the love, the dynamics of the relationship are forever altered, with most other important issues taking second place to the illness and being left unresolved.

no blame, old man, but pain the same,
no blame but you hurt me.
you the man, watching me watching you
watching that child too soon come of age.
too late you listened, long gone was I
to walk a lonely, trembling road alone.

the memories are fading, but the bandages remain,
wrapped tightly around that Child of mine.
lost then, though all saw him smiling,
lost now, though yearning to be seen,
still mutely tearing at hooded emotions,
running in circles,
absurdly innocent even now.

Your Pain ruled us all, consumed us all,
we nurses danced obediently in attendance,
only gaining approval
by deference to Your Pain.
and finally, it took you
but left us, with nobody to attend, no attack to defend.
only your spirit swoops now, encouraging, pleading,
for Your Pain is long gone, yet my Child's remains.

no blame, old man, but pain the same.
no blame but pain the same.

A Moment

There is a moment, a defining moment, which strikes your very core in its clarity and its power: the moment where you realise the love you have been searching for and believing in for your entire life, is real. Its essence stays with you always, imprinted as a memory upon your very cells of perfection in its most staggering form, of the simultaneous expanding and contracting of all you have known, or will ever know.

To experience that moment is to understand all others.

it was just a moment, a second,
a blink of the eyes of time

but I remember that moment,
forever scorched on my senses,
for it was the moment I knew

that first sight of her, you see,
the first sight stays with me,
superimposed upon my life

it was on a rock
and I was burning,
I looked up and saw magnificence
and was alone no more

on that rock
her beauty stood, unadorned,
her aura haloed by a sinking sun,
both unashamed of their radiance

a rock, just a rock, but it was
that rock
and *that* moment
the sea crashed inside of me

and the sea had known
and the rock knew too,
but we knew more

for in that moment, on that rock

life began...

and ended

Changing Days

Almost without us realising, life moves on from the dreams and possibilities of our youth through the work-filled, child-rearing days of our twenties and thirties, until we wake up one morning and we are middle-aged. Though reminded so often by parents and elders to enjoy those seasons, for they pass so quickly, the realisation that they have indeed passed still shocks each of us. One cloudy day we notice we are holding those unfulfilled dreams, unrequited loves and compromised desires that we believed would never be ours.

the smells that teased,
sights to seize your breath,
sounds exploding the day.
where lie those moments of wonder?

the adrenalin that coursed through veins,
the appetite to pluck at stars,
the dauntless daring to go beyond.
where are the hopes that danced in dreams?

the smiling eyes and aching sides,
the empty bottles of last night,
those life-long friends that slipped away.
who silenced the laughter?

the shivers of delight from the merest caress,
the breakers of passion crashing,
the orgasms of being alive.
where does pleasure hide now?

the blind conviction of its imminence,
the anticipation of a heat sublime,
that simple belief it lay waiting, somewhere.
when did the search for love stumble?

innocence slides silently away
and fear creeps up and bites,
solitude becomes our company
as the blazing fires of desire die.
when did life's chalice cease to shine?

where have you gone,
bright coveted dreams and deepest longings?

were you ever real?

Knowing

It is easy to be a holy man on top of a mountain. It is only in the rigours of life do we genuinely find a profound sense of our self and our Spirituality. And it is when we are tested to the limit, in those times when we feel most alone and most confused, our real knowing of ourselves and the world around us truly happens. Sometimes, carried in a seminal moment, knowledge ascends from being just a belief to fact, changing integrally the way we live.

The ruins of the Château at Rennes, o'er
Looking such lush, sleeping valleys,
Stand proud against time, nature, man and church:
Truth to out, one day.
A Gnostic I became on that windswept hill
Whilst wandering ancient Cathar lands,
Where hushed mountains give silent witness.

… The knowledge given may never be denied,
Nor may you say, you did not know …
Those words once said, returned,
With that fine clarity of understanding,
As rare as the dream both caught and remembered,
As clear and true as a child's tear.

Believing becomes Knowing; faith: wisdom,
Who you are is not who you were, a moment ago
As realisation breaks confusion's shroud.
The simple beauty of the Deity,
The polarity of truth versus dogma
As opposite as a butterfly to a paper plane,
A flower to a plastic cup,
Love, to lust's fleeting embrace,
Truth, to a lie.

Strangely, it came not from meeting a man
Who knew, but from meeting a man
Who knew nothing at all;
Not from a man who had lost all ego, but
An ego that had lost all trace of the man.

Truth, in all its lucidness, unadorned,
With all complexities abandoned,
Is more beautiful than the eyes could ever see,
Or ears hear, fingers touch.

And as the pendulum of reality swings,
It rests in Knowing, and sways no more.

Picture Show

Photographs from the camera in our minds pile up in a corner, images collected and forgotten until a trigger, a flash, has them pouring before our eyes, and before our hearts. This ability of our memory is the pictorial account of our life, a hoard of treasure we can bury or keep accessible, depending on the emotion attached to the images. The nature of their privacy enables us an unabridged personal freedom, though at times this very isolation suppresses an opportunity for their truth to be shared with, and believed by, another.

one hundred thousand images of her
swallow-swoop my mind,
I gaze too long at one
and another smiles, beguiled

or belly-laughs, head thrown back

or breath-sucked gasps in wonder

or sways away, boot-clad naked, red feather in her hair

this secret hoard of pictures of her
blitzing my days, teasing the nights
a members-only private show,
my top-shelf magazine
to finger through and fantasise

I gorge on an orgy of these epitomes
as she wonders what I see
when my eyes capture her face once more;
that breath before the lens clicks
and her doubts slide in

methinks she thinks it's her body I crave
and yes, oh yes
those sculptured breasts, come-hither neck and flooded thighs
loose these loins
and that seat of such sublime design spreads gently down
to mesmerise

but it is her face
I long for
and linger on,
the place wherein her beauty truly lies

if only she could see

Unremembered

When we step into someone else's inner world we bring our own sense of truth with us, a different slant from their own, a truth that may be difficult to accept since its subjectivity is often in conflict with what they themselves believe to be true. We all run, but the sadness is when we sacrifice a future well-being to escape a raw immediacy.

this stir of a dragon moonrise
this taste of bitter-sweet love
this beauty we leave gasping through
an unheard wail in the darkness

such love, my love
etched harsh with deliverance
a strange and torrid gift
this power of stealing hearts

I am the gap
the wilderness

the truth that pulls you away

Ask Yourself

It is the nature of romantic love that we all believe we have loved and been loved. It is the honesty of our hearts that bids us question. Relationship is such a changing state that frequently we compromise on those things which are acutely important to us, and then we wonder why we feel unappreciated and unfulfilled. If a relationship is wrong it cannot be made right by denying our needs, it is only made more unsatisfying. But in love, compromise is not at the expense of self, rather it *embraces* self, and without embracing self, we cannot surrender self.

Maybe we need to ask ourselves earlier and more often, if the relationship we are in really encompasses all that we believe we deserve, and desire.

Ask yourself.
Have you loved as you dreamed of loving?
Where the air they exhale
Is the air you breathe
And their juices your only sustenance?

Ask yourself.
Have you bathed in their bath to submerge in their smell,
Or crawled on cold floors to find a hair left behind?
Found pride in subservience,
Surrendered self and watched dignity borne
With ego nailed to humility's cross?

Ask yourself.
Have you sold your soul to love?

Where religion only worships the Divine-other.
Where their dreams sparkle star-like in your night sky.
Have you unbarred the windows to your secret thoughts
And seen absolution smile,
Nailing fear to honesty's cross?

Ask yourself.
Have you been loved as you dreamed?
When beauty is a gift and not a threat,
When anger rouses desire
And every fantasy reflects their image.
Have you gorged on their pleasure and lay sated,
Have you held emotions beyond passion,

Beyond belief?

So you have loved?
Are you sure?

I was,
Until her.

Pleas

All too often we walk past the doors that open themselves to us, deciding the levels of difficulty they will give passage to somehow outweigh the depth of knowledge or beauty they will also place at out feet. It is not enough to feel comfortable in the skin of our subjective truths. It is only in following a path that explores these beliefs about ourselves, which shows both their light and their shadows, that we can begin to understand the false images we cling to.

Take your pleas
Self-righteous e-s
And let it be-s
Go get your fix
Of fickle friends
And young boys' tease

Like a drunk
Boring sober
I prefer your poems
Than your realities

Rejection hurts
Feeds my disease

But most of all
We dribbled our chance
To walk our talk
And be our fantasies

Spilled Wine

It is easy in sexual love, or lust, to believe you are an unselfish lover, or that your partner is not. And so it is with life. Perhaps we are the poorest judge of our unselfishness, or the lack of it. Perhaps we need to delve more deeply behind our partner's spoken and unspoken words. Perhaps we need to care as much for others' needs as we do our own.

You are so selfish, she said
As she wrapped her legs around him.
You are so selfish, she moaned
As he slipped slowly inside her.
You are so selfish, she groaned
As her back arched demandingly under him.
You are so selfish, she shouted
As her body tensed with anticipation.
You are so selfish, she wailed
As her body shuddered with orgasm.
You are so selfish, she screamed
As she climaxed, again and again.

You are so selfish, she sighed
As she prepared for more pleasure.
You are so selfish, she growled
As he thrust deeply into her.
You are so selfish, she roared
As her body writhed around his hardness.
You are so selfish, she yelled
As she climbed to another peak.

You are so selfish, she whined
As she lay gorged on her own pleasure.
You are so selfish, she snapped
When he stopped to rest awhile.
You are so selfish, she spat
As she slapped him on his cheek.
You are so selfish, she sneered
As he backed away, bewildered.

You are so selfish, she cried
As he left.

Lake of Love

The language of the heart speaks only to empower, to embrace, to honour. Through its words, its passion, the gentle tone of its soft voice, it guides you into a sanctuary, a place to lay your head as its waters rinse you free of the past. One would think this was enough.

You led me to the lake
Of love, and washed me clean.

You swept me to the hall
Of dreams, and watched me dance.

You heaved me up to a cloud
Of truth, and soothed my doubts.

You reached for me from
A distant realm, and dared me believe.

You pulled me to a place
Of freedom, and forced my fear to flee.

You enticed me with the food
Of fantasy, and begged me feed.

You wished me to the well
Of desire, and bid me drown.

We washed together
In the lake of love

But asked for more.

Little Bird

When someone stands before us, disrobed and naked in their brokenness, love witnesses their entire breadth and does not cower. For it is in our acceptance that we help loosen their false bindings of shame, of guilt and of fear, encouraging their own determination to sever them. And if wellness leads them to paths where we are not, we honour freedom in its highest form by praying their migration is through clear blue skies.

hidden from prying sight
slumped with broken wings
and feathers bloodied by the battle
fragile unseen skeleton barely covered
smashed

behind frightened eyes you looked at me
daring me to believe you could survive
as if somehow you were to blame
for this torment by another's shame

wiping the bloody ashes away
binding the brittle bones so gently
caressing them with insufficient words
you almost surrendered to me, but

the touch and go of life hovered
and bare feet crossed broken glass
before belief would at last intervene
and the wounds would stop their killing

and now
time has filled your feathers bright
the bitter scars have healed
your head grows proud, eyes unafraid
as they meet the truth you always were:
soft singer of sweet soliloquy

I know you will fly away one day
back to your own perhaps
but see you have shone a light so bright
it pierced my very soul

and I like to think we will meet again

somewhere

Cognisance

Sometimes it is just a hint, a faint intimation of a recognition that reaches beyond our physical form. At other times, or even just once, there is more than recognition. There is a distant, hazy memory of another life, another time spent together.

were you always there

waiting

was it just my eyes

closed?

or did the distant drums need a different rhythm

to hear our heart song call

again.

the beat of tender past

heaving out of hooded shroud,

resisting the time-warp

of mirrored memories

and sofa-sat synchronicity.

then I knew,

I knew you recognised me,

again.

Ouch

When our heart is entwined with another's and the relationship fails, the loss spreads out and pours over into all parts of our lives. Our receiving of the great immensity of love shifts entirely in meaning, for it is in the subtle changes, the tiny absences, the nakedness of a life without love is truly known. Perhaps we become so preoccupied within the drama of loving, that the details rippling in the undercurrent slowly drift away from our attention.

sinking searing belly-wrenching pain
of one hundred million kisses missed

whispered words silently screamed
of a silver ring fingered through eternity

bleeding tongues tasting invisible wounds
of minds confused in heart's stirring stew

the bathroom's bare
no hair on my brush
just the remorseless reminder
from empty pillows
of our fuck-'em-all nights

roller-coastering emotional savagery
of dreams left desert dry
the stars missing in soulless skies
of colour-drained hue

the kitchen's clean
no pans in the sink
only memory's stain on pristine sheets
of petal-filled nights and
feathered words

throat-tearing silence hangs hopelessly
unforgiving of songs sung and swayed

this is the afterbirth
this is the pain

of this love's triumph

Intimate Strangers

Through sudden shifts in awareness at times like these, we have all experienced the intense recognition of a stranger, someone out of reach of our conscious memory. These instances grab you in their rarity, as though time expands and slows down, and suddenly you are aware of something more subtle, more implicit flowing and emanating. There becomes a frame of time in which the mind seems to drop away and a deeper sense of perception cushions your touch, your sensitivity to sound...

You are unknown to me, yet you stand remembered
As some strange twist of my senses
Rouses with the memory of you.
I cannot tear my eyes away
From eyes that dart and laugh and flash.
And then, behind a smile a glimpse
Of other times I seem to understand.
Have we met once? A time ago
Across a bar, on a plane, in a dream perhaps?
Were we lovers once? In a life somewhere
That quickens, rustles, awakens
As we move uneasily in this room as strangers.

Have I stroked your face, have I?
Have I lain with you, skin against skin?
Felt you naked and curled beside me…
How can I stir these thoughts in you?
What look, what word, would slip a memory of me,
Would leave your eyes free from hiding,
Would catch our truth in this meaningless mélange?

You look at me, but I lower my eyes,
Unable to hold your gaze,
Yet hoping that you trembled, too, in this re-awakening.
I meet your eyes, again,
To see you look through me, beyond me,
As if I were not even there.

Did you not recognise me at all?
Am I just a face to you, a stranger?

I am just a face to you.
A stranger.

And you never knew.

Dirty Habit

Sexual abuse of children is only just beginning to be fully acknowledged in our society and is still far from being understood or dealt with effectively. Societally, we appear unable to accept our collective responsibility for the violation of the countless children we fail to protect.

Organised Religion has many crimes to answer for. But its covering up and blatant denial of the thousands of children who have suffered unimaginable abuse at the hands of those who hide behind the Church's closed doors, pretending to practise God's love, is the most hideous and unforgivable of them all.

They glide across the room, those monks in black Habits,
The cross they wear hangs powerfully, righteously,
Representing the God they serve, the love they offer,
And the young boy lays his trust upon that cross,
In those men, for they are holy, teachers,
Surrogate fathers so revered, beyond suspicion.
Respected priests.

Molested by the Daytime Habit, fondled by the Night-time Habit
As he fails to protect the darkness, that time when fear
Grips every child and their parents should be near.
Alone in his bed, holding his breath, the boy listens,
Heart pounding as the Night-time Habit prowls,
Breathing again if the footsteps fade and the Habit floats away.

Does God do this too, he wonders, staring at the altar,
The place where the Habits group and perform their rituals,
Piously praying before preaching of love and compassion.
And then later in the Confessional, he is the sinner,
And must seek their penance for crimes unlike their own,
Their sick secrets, all hidden in this charade,
To rip at his heart as he stares at the Virgin.

The ultimate sacrilege, the cruellest blasphemy
Is this perversion they perpetrate, hidden by the veneration
They adulate, to mask the innocence they contaminate.
The Habits that don't indulge know those who can't resist,
And are guilty too, for their silence sentences him
To the shackles of their sordid lairs.

con.

In the name of the Father they seduce the children,
These role models of Saint and teacher, brother and man,
This abuse of God, abuse of power, abuse of trust
All defiling the sacred innocence of a child:
Religion, manhood, fatherhood, sexuality all violated,
Tossed into the abyss to be buried deep.

As they hide behind that Habit,
That depraved, dirty habit of theirs,
The stench in which they wallow is worse than any other.
How can they believe in what they preach
When they practise such profanities?
How do they sleep at night
Knowing what they are?

We sleep with God, they say.

They sleep alone, I fear.

Alone.

Breakdown

Catalysed by a complete loss of love for oneself, a breakdown is the inability to both support a life *and* manage the effects of inner torment. For someone who has not experienced a breakdown, it is impossible to understand. For someone who has, it is impossible to describe. There are appalling but inevitable conclusions delivered by sexual abuse, or abuse of any kind, because the damage it inflicts upon the children it tortures is on so many levels.

Communities wonder why some teenagers become drug addicts or criminals, why some adults become abusers or alcoholics, or why doctors' surgeries are full of people struggling to cope with their lives. If we were only able to look into some of the childhoods, have a degree of insight into the experiences shaping those very people we judge so quickly, perhaps we would be more compassionate and more forgiving.

I realised something was wrong just moments before it began,
But it was too late, not knowing then I was never to return.
All choices were removed as something far more powerful than I
Took over,
Isolating me on a burning tightrope as the impending doom
Began to form and threaten, the knot in my stomach tightening,
Hands moistening, breath quickening.
I could not look back: that time had gone, forever.

Onward I went, deeper and deeper into the void,
Somewhere beyond imagination,
A place where love did not exist, truth and time disappearing
As I waited, paralysed, unable to hold on, to grip,
To halt the vacuum sucking me further and further
Into the hell expecting me, waiting to torture all I had held safe,
And caught in the mouth of the guillotine I could not move,
Transfixed,
Watching the terror of the waking nightmare unfold in my mind's eye,
Incapable now of stopping the revulsion from attacking,
Each invasion more hideous, terrifying,
Than the one before, one appalling hallucination
After the other, no respite, breathless, my eyes darting,
Frantic, desperate to know from where the next assault would hit,
Defenceless,
Cowering as they came swooping bat-like, shivering in fear
Of this vortex of terror, guzzling me in, in, down, pleading for it to stop,
Please,
Please God, what is happening, the words pant through the dryness of my
Mouth, I believe I am dying, wanting to live, afraid to die,
Let me live! My mind explodes with the panic, all control
Stolen, sick with fear of the darkness impaling me,
Recoiling from the obscenities inhaling me, swallowing me down
Into a nether world, an abyss, Hades,
Ghouls diving into me, picking at my flesh, breaking my bones,
Every inch of my body, my mind, attacked, eaten, broken, smashed,
Peeled, splintered, gouged,
The pain swamping me as I lay screaming, silently, pleading into the dark,
How can I stop it…? When will it end…? Someone, anyone, God,
The devil… Help me!…. Please, help me!!!….. Help, me!!!!!!!!!!

con.

No help came.
I staggered around, beating the air, the invisible attackers,
I crawled about the floor like a rabid animal, then curled myself,
Foetus-like, trying to find a womb to hide in,
Crying out incoherently into the quietness, the loudest quietness,
Such deafening silence, begging to know who I was, where reality went,
Time passing in seconds of seething terror, minutes of lucid madness,
Hours of utter horror.
I kept talking to myself, my voice unrecognisable, trying
To rationalise the irrational, understand the implausible,
I knew I was losing, drifting, exhausted, travelling now beyond fear,
Beyond reason,
The life-force sucked from me, assiduously, lost, lost in a place
Impossible to understand, with no way out but to die…
Death by now my only friend.

He was waiting,
Waiting to take me from this place that had stripped me
Of all sanity,
Killing me slowly as he savoured the final
Violations, indignities, suffering….
And I welcomed Him.

My final memory is of reaching out to Death,
And gratefully taking his hand.

Shifting Sands

In the wake of the frightening isolation we face during a breakdown, in whatever form the collapse of Self takes, is the realisation that our lives have changed forever. All that we had held to be true alters, and depression, drug dependency, alcoholism and addiction are the traps that wait seductively to ensnare us. Until we have experienced the wretched loneliness of emotional disintegration, a place so absent of love lies beyond our imagination.

Wondering when the darkness will disappear
A weary soldier treads another barren land,
Trapped in the tunnels of his sorrow,
He is his only friend
And enemy,
His life a wave exploding on the rocks,
Retreating with a hanged pause, this momentary hush
Before the next fall,
His essence long caught in its watery tomb.

A part from the world to which he was born,
The hook on which to hang their hopes,
The sometimes lover of such serenade…
The dark horse that stands aloof,
The loner of whom they suspected all,
A black sheep who broke man's rules.

Love tempts in seductive slivers, selective
In her timing, never choosing to stay,
For morning brings the shadows to share his bed
And torment his day.
His net of thoughts drags through memories,
Catching pangs of pain, aches of loss from battles fought,
Whilst pleasures hide in shells of tangled recollections
And the haze of hell-raised nights.

The shifting sands of his sanity soldier on
As Death, the shadow of a sunnier day,
Calls out again to slice the head from his longing,
His longing to belong, this stranger from a lost crusade
Fighting an unnamed war,
His scarred body searching to find the place
He once called home,
But never can.

Faceless Shadow

Mental illness is society's last taboo but until we learn to unravel the sequence of events that often lead up to it, or become more educated about its potential gene connection, then we will continue to shy away from it. There is such a contradiction in our sympathising with physical damage we can easily see, and our turning away in fear from emotional or psychological illness. Our society is happy to question why some people seem so unable to love, or be loved, yet is failing to prepare itself for the answers.

It waits for him come morning light,
Looming dark to opening eyes,
And his heart knots from knowing
In the peace of sleep, it did not die.
This shadow of an unforgiving night.

It follows him, mocking his day,
Hissing into thoughts,
A faceless ravenous parasite
Craving more and more
His fear and shame and dread.
This shadow of an unforgiving night.

Voracious vampire of dignity,
Lies dripping from its fangs
It promises to devour him,
To slowly tear its way inside
And gorge on the rotting feast
It bred.
This shadow of an unforgiving night.

It slinks behind as he staggers to bed,
Taunting his feeble attempt at escape,
Fills to full height as he lays his head,
To tower a breath away
From his wearied sense.
This shadow of an unforgiving night.

This shadow of an unforgiving night.

The Fear

If forced to look inwards amidst the chaos, down to where the shadows lie in each of us, we start to identify the reasons and understand the sequential nature of our lives. In uncovering the causes of our fears we discover the strength to overcome them, and here begin our first steps towards freedom and our return to love.

The axe split the child in two,
One half to face the world, one to hide.

The broken glass ripped out the eyes
To never see again the sights they saw.

The teeth were uprooted one by one
To disable the desire to bite.

The tearing out of the tongue
Strangled the scream not screamed.

The genitals were cut away
To exorcise the cause of the lie.

The hammer smashed the skull
To destroy the memories.

The heart impaled itself upon the knife
To bleed itself dry.

Killing the child
Killed the remnants of a wounded self.

The Fear was the fear of all these things,
Yet just symbols dying to be decoded;
Dramatic, as all other signs passed unnoticed,
Desperate, for it was the last frantic cry

From within

For help.

Hairy Beast

Love, in whatever form, criss-crosses the paths of our lives even in those times when we exist unaware of its presence. Its beauty is shown no more powerfully than when it is given unconditionally and reciprocation is not sought. And as we try to pull ourselves out of the darkness it is often the most unexpected hand that reaches out to grasp our own.

In the shadows the hairy beast moves.
Slowly,
Threatening, lurking,
Its footsteps silently haunting
The dead hero.
Parsifal feels him but knows him not - and
Whispers naught, should anyone hear -
But alone in the throng, trembles,
His unknown enemy stirring again.

The hideous damsel appears, smiling,
Yet knowingly mirrors the hairy beast
That lurks.

Parsifal recoils: wounded, confused, accused,
For the candle she holds shows Him
Within him.

The shadow is born into light,
The hairy beast is stilled, chains removed:
Only the prison was its darkness.

Fear confronted creates truth, perhaps
An ally to be, no less –
As she is and was before

And knew.

Fragment

When a child suffers abuse emotionally, physically or sexually, they are incapable of understanding why. In continued abuse, a child may create places in their mind and emotions to escape the confusion and pain, an extension of the natural self-protective measures we all take. But the cruel danger of this defence is the detachment of those places from the whole.

If these fragments are not gathered and re-integrated, a child's desperate need for separation from their turmoil develops into adults disassociated from some part of their emotional selves.

instinctively
my soul prepared for the incoming pain,
embracing itself against the impact,
but a fragment fractured deep into the chaos
to wander aimlessly alone

a shard of pain in the pit of my sadness,
I felt him always, this fragment of myself,
a stranger I ran from into oblivion, to gorge
on feasts of pleasure and numb his presence,
my rampant ego chasing shadows in the wastelands
as he waited, forgotten

how could he survive that quicksand of memories
where we both sank without trace,
all those mislaid years,
his strangled voice deafened by
the bedlam of my emotions

one calm day in the wake of ambiguity,
long since the damage done,
I caught his tiny voice in a heart searching for meaning,
and like a dream not quite grasped
I glimpsed him

his small hand reached for mine,
my heart pounding for this fragment of my Self
coming home:
the child I was and the man he will be

we smile, a smile of recognition,
as we meet for the first time.

Bureau D'Amour

There is a calling we hear and move towards when we search for love. Sometimes it is as though we stand in a deep valley, with the voice echoing between mountains and disguising its place of origin, and we pause before our next step, hesitant and unsure. But we carry on, always hoping that the hills may drop away, that the land will unfurl into the open space of clarity. It is here that love perceives its partner, in the distance, approaching like the weather. It is here that love meets itself.

this is a moment of belly-skin-touching awe
the death-rattle to a lifetime's yearning
an extraordinary breathing-while where
love's endless search for itself

ends.

cradled in the bosom of satin skin's sanctuary
the door to our dungeon of disbelieved words
now hangs open forever

old souls embrace
freedom's dreams rebound from eternity
saliva-wetted words
become liquid lipless kisses
and shame's claws release their grip

eyes meet knowing eyes
chest meets heaving breasts

past doubts and aches

melt and drain away

through open thighs

and only reverence remains

Cocktails

Sometimes the ridiculousness of the mating game makes us smile, at other times it can make us feel that we have arrived somehow from another planet. But brought up on this one, we learn to play the game, though still aware somewhere of the manipulation taking place and the untruths told, the suspect compliments we give and are given, the absurdity of this designer meat market, and the ever distancing our role in it takes us from love.

As the monotonous hum of the party rises
and compulsory prattle fills the air with expectation,
he looks out across the crowded room
with a resigned quiet desolation,
as a snowflake, stranded on desert sands,
eyes the rising sun in anxious resignation,
or a dancer missing the music's cue
and not knowing what to do, is lost in hesitation;
an actor's forgotten lines, frozen in time;
an embarrassing ejaculation.

The people move oblivious to his lack of ease
as tortured lips squeeze merry conversation,
inane mutterings masking the dis-ease,
a slow death through verbal cremation.

His darting eyes search for a stairway to flee to,
away from this public self-flagellation,
a quiet corner to hide in, confide in,
unnoticed amidst the heaving affectation.

Safely backed against the wall
he surveys the seasoned rituals of recreation,
where tired lies and fertile minds
prepare to pretend aroused fascination.

The seducers seduce and the unavailable accept,
strangers linked through wide-eyed dedication
as neutral comments carry sly conundrums
of obvious solicitation,
where pride's persistent appetite for compliment
ignores the oft rehearsed salacious insinuation,
and hungry enough for any flattery
responds with smiling desperation.

con.

As insobriety loosens the purest of intents
and the running time nags of potential humiliation,
another night alone! the fear of sleeping on their own
flings them into the fray with renewed anticipation.

The games gather urgency,
the rites focus with increasing flirtation,
closer and closer, the looks deepen, no fear now
of the unspoken implication, the blatant manipulation:
the casts have been flung and the foolish take the fly
with unashamed vocation.

From his corner, he tires of the games,
and as he makes to leave the growing machination,
his line tightens.

The Battlefield

The finely tuned coordination of our emotions can often resemble more of a war zone where we fight ourselves or someone else, where our inner dis-ease creates a threatening environment of unrevealed thoughts and fears and lost dreams. The less glamorous side of romantic love is that it heightens and magnifies our vulnerabilities and insecurities, and presents us with the same battles we try to flee.

And yet this is, too, the gift of love because through this very exposing do we begin to make well, do we begin to still the struggle. Perhaps it can only be from a place of such stillness that we see the full extent of our previous chaos.

I lie in a netherland of wakefulness,
Images tossing and teasing me
As my restless mind probes and plays,
A hamster's wheel of thoughts that
Circles in the quiet:
This solitude unique to man,
A time alone with his judge in a private court.

I wait for sleep and think of you.
Awareness flowers in responsibility's garden,
Love waters the growing shoots of wisdom that
Flourish now in my spiritual soil, a once infertile ground.
I gaze into the mirror of my life's life,
Wiping through the steam of my experience,
Looking for some faint reflection of my integrity
Until, slowly, conscience appears, reflected,
Flushed calm by a smile.
The raging battlefield of emotions that roared
Lies seemingly at rest, conflicts stilled,
Barely smoking embers the faint reminder
Of the fire, the quests accepted, the journeys completed,
The acquiescence to ones yet to come.

Unavailable for love, it shadowed me.
When I would turn, the shadow moved, eclipsed,
With none to blame than I.
Or them.
And now, as the pain and ecstasy of your voice
Hangs heavy in my heart,
Love's essence persists
And I can feel you, hear you, touch you as though
You lay beside me, curled inseparably inside me.

At last my night's journey draws close,
My spirit to wander,
To fly to freedom's resting place.
And as I slip to sleep,
I feel you waiting.

If the Truth Be Known

Through love we see the beauty of another in its fullness. But in that same love, and in the mirror it offers us, we equally see the sometimes brutal truth about ourselves.

Your beauty is unbroken by life
Its oak tree strength
Proud
And unbent

As is my love for you

My beauty is bleached and fraying
With a willow tree sway
Of doubts
And insecurities

As is my love for me

Will She?

Someone once said that love brings up anything unlike itself to be healed. To walk in the environment it shapes around us requires our complete faith, for so exposed are we to its elements, to its storms and its droughts, to its tremors and the dark of its nightfall. Jealousy, suspicion, doubt, all creep into the openness in ourselves we have lain bare by opening our hearts.

My heart is held within her breath,
Hanging, swooning, soaring, sinking,
Bungy-jumping into Paradise

And Back.

Her coiled finger brings it galloping stallion-proud,
Her back-turned silence sends it cowering foal-sad,
Unsure of its world,
Unsteady.

She asked for this heart
And I gave it,
Yet a history of slow death shadows her
And haunts me.

Will she,
Will she?

Will she finger-slip this flooding heart
Into freefall,

Go take her song and sing it elsewhere?

Will she?

Is she?

Beguiled

At times in our lives, if we are lucky, we have a relationship with someone who seems to fulfil all the criteria we thought we desired in a lover. And yet some indiscernible little thing is missing. Everything we see in them and experience with them should fulfil what we were searching for, and in our confusion as to why they are not enough we realise we neither truly know nor understand them; nor ourselves.

behind that smile
languid eyes
and lips that follow me
such beautiful words
muse
your tenderness

gentle whisperer
of fearless silence
and sweet caress

intimate dancer
of alluring love
and doe-shy glance

wounded heart
saddened soul
and bruised-blue innocence.

O gracious love,

who are you?

Sussed

Just as we can puzzle about how our dreams and expectations somehow slipped away unnoticed, we can also fool ourselves about the happiness of our lives. Material comfort and a stress-free existence can mask the compromises we have made and the joys we no longer feel. An unforeseen blessing comes through someone reminding us of all we once dreamed and what we have imperceptibly forgotten. And that ageing need not necessarily be an end to the beliefs that once inspired us.

I lay on the lounger of middle-aged spread
carefully smoothing the wrinkles of doubt,
cupped my hands behind a self-satisfied head
and spread my legs before a red, maturing sun:

It was sussed. This business of life.

And then she whispered... "But do you see the beauty?"

Intuitly, tenderly, she uncovered my innocence
long veiled by experience's pride.

Bravely, wildly, she embraced my desire
defeated by cold shackles of shame.

And, slowly, released the catch of a cynical cage
where worship lay waiting.

And then she smiled... "And do you see *your* beauty?"

It was not sussed, this business of life,
lying behind invisible blinkers,
reality numbed
by some creeping, emotionless security.

In seeing the world
through the frosted glass of compromise,
I had lost my clarity of belief
and lived a lesser life
than my dreams deserved.

I was not old, I just looked with old eyes
I was not blind, I had only forgotten how to see

So, thank you, priestess of perception,
these new eyes fit me well.

But will they always look at you?

Belly-Backed

From the hundreds of intricacies weaving through a relationship, there are those, delicious and rare, that penetrate the very core of connection, which seem to breathe its essence. And beyond there, amidst the lustre, lies the single embodiment of them all, the wordless communication of union. It is this which leaves the indelible mark of its absence.

'tis not the lovemaking I miss so much
or soul food lovingly prepared
nor jasmine baths casually shared

'tis not wandering upon the cliffs
or the re-awakened mysteries our bodies once wove
nor unholy communion in a sunlit cove

'tis not the sofa tête-à-têtes
or flickering candles in opal eyes
nor heart-slapping, soaring, emotional highs

no,

'tis not little fingers knowingly interlocked
or the secrets and shadows unmasked by this lover
nor the hidden notes of love left to uncover

'tis not razored nights of rose-petalled love
or coffee coloured anemones that made us smile
nor lips that took our breath away for a while

no, not even those,

'tis the subtle scent of your neck slip-sliding into sleep
and velvet skin stirring in the dance of one another's dreams

'tis waking in the night and finding you

I miss so much

Walking The Truth

We have a choice. We can await love and honour its arrival. Or we can await love and dishonour it by carving its edges to fit our own design. Every place other than a place of love is, ultimately, selfish because without love there is only ego.

We exploit love so unashamedly it is a wonder it doesn't give up on us all.

love is not what you say
but what you do.
it is the deed, not the word.
it is the gesture, not the thought.
it is the embrace freely given, not a touch withheld.

love is not promising to stay
and leaving.

your empty phrases
are but one drop of water
in love's deep ocean,
one blade of grass
in love's endless pastures,
one lone star in love's infinite universe.

so do not mouth love
if all you seek
are self desires satisfied.
do not vow love
if you choose not to hear
its cries to listen.
and do not sing this song of love
as some sardonic serenade.

for when you speak of love so lightly,
you abuse it,
and me.

Deer Woman

Love comes our way in many guises and though we may try intently to receive it, ultimately it can only offer itself before us. Love from another will not force a path into our hearts. It rests with the love in our own to find a path out.

Your tears tear into his heart,
The sobbing torments his throbbing guilt -
Forgive the flames of your anguish, try,
For they crush him too.
Oh, Precious Woman,
Gentle as a snowflake upon my tongue,
How do you not see
It was always this way?
Those sharp, slicing knives of his past
Carved the prison of his future,
Freed for a time by this wonder of you.
In waiting long to be so loved,
A desperate hand was pitched
To grasp the beauty of your soul.

But my grip broke,
Of course,
And I slipped.

This pain, these tears
Were always waiting,
Their ghostly presence
Behind adoring, shining eyes,
And so cry, sweet love,
Purge your anger, softly rock the cradle of your loss.
But as what blossomed falls to Winter-sleep,
Consider this:
Rather you then, than you now?

Ménage

Relationships all over the world are often stopped from even beginning at all, be it for racial, gender or cultural reasons, or for any one of the infinite reasons as to why two people in love can not be together. The pain of finding love that has an inevitable end brings so heavy a sorrow, that the weight is sometimes as oppressive as the pleasure is light. But, perhaps, we gain more in accepting the possibility of falling, than in making no attempt at all to scale its heights.

unspoken thoughts of unwritten words
in unsent letters
of disallowed love.
in secrets and lies freedom dies
hiding in shadows of whispers

but I don't care

I have lived in your world
with your layers of laws
and your folds of fears
and I didn't fit in.

tell me,
were you to feel divine, sublime
blessed and chosen,
were you shown heaven -
would you turn back and run away?

who can deny or judge me
who will shy away from me
before they see
and understand this love,
this magnificent ménage?

in these loves' incarnation
I stand at the foothills of enlightenment
innocent, unclothed and unafraid
for joy flows from love
as easily as the dance from the dancer
and without it life has no meaning.

if you could see what I see
feel the wonder I feel
hear the song written in *my* heart
then you would know heaven
perfection
deliverance

and you would meet your soul.

We Live In A Dream

There is something in the experience of true love which separates you from the world, not in terms of superiority, but in the heart finding a different rhythm and the movement of time becoming immeasurable from the turning of the sun. Beliefs, emotions, priorities, all get turned on their head and feet fall upon fresh ground as our circle of life widens.

We live in a dream
You and I
Where the sun rains and the clouds burn
And glorious arias become monastic chants
Where the past is the present and the future's guillotine

Where agony surfaces in ecstasy's flood

We live in a dream where
What is, isn't
Where who we are stops us being
Who we are
Where us is more
And I am less

'Tis a dream where fortune favours the fearful
And the brave fail
Where people are strangers and spirits known
Where walls listen and friends close their ears

Aye, a dream, this journey of ours
With love the only power
Not money
Not success
And age holds only irrelevance
When wisdom speaks

One look enacts the play complete
One word the book
As long, convoluted conversations
Bring no further understanding
Dark memories are forgotten
And the unseen, seen
And those long arms of truth embrace the hurt
And won't let go

con.

A dream

Where touch invokes wonder before lust
Where sex is sacred
And not a fast food fuck
Or a solitary toss into the recesses of the mind

Where nothing is forbidden
And no rules apply

Where I knew you before you were you
And loved you before I was me

Where time rushes by so slowly

Death

Caught up in our mortality, believing the idea that our existence dies with us, we lose the meaning of death. We have only to widen our perspective, soften the barriers around our senses and truth whispers through the quiet. Our bodies are shown as a medium, a channel for a journeying soul, and the only real death becomes that which suspends expression of the heart.

to live is to love

and to love is to be without fear

of anything

you do not survive love

you do not die of love

because death is not dying:

living without love is

Us

It is in our separation as individuals, lovers, communities, societies and from our planet, that we lose touch with and sight of our oneness. Every cause has an effect, just as each action we undertake as individuals affects someone, somewhere. In the waves of oneness we feel our connection to love. In their absence, we wage war as families, couples, groups and nations, and threaten each other and our planet.

There is you

And me

And Us

A physical Us

An emotional Us

A human Us

Yet forever, there has been

A timeless Us

A Divine Us

A Universal Us

There has always been just Us

One Us

There is no you

And me

Only Us

Icebergs

we think of ourselves as ordinary and then we discover how extraordinary we can be to someone who adores us; we think of ourselves as icebergs floating in a sea of self-contained isolation, and then we discover how magnificent we can be to someone who cherishes the entirety of our being; we see ourselves made ugly by our doubts and insecurities, and then we discover how beautiful we can be to someone whose own uncertainties allow them to see us unconditionally; we think of ourselves as plain and uninteresting until we discover how desirable we can be to someone who worships us; we think romantic, idealistic love exists only in poems and daydreams until we discover someone who believes in love as we do;
we think we are alone and then we discover another,
and in each other we discover
our destiny.